Discoveries

Discoveries

Finding Life's Special Joys
By Ruth E. Mohring
Illustrated by
Barbara White

Hallmark Editions

DISCOVERIES

Finding something is one
of life's great adventures...

It can happen
in a fleeting moment
when you see a falling star...

Or on a long journey
when you visit a strange land.

Sometimes you can find
little things that bring
small moments of delight--
the right button
for a buttonless shirt...

A shiny new penny among the old...

A wiggly worm in the soft earth--
simple finds that you've seldom told.

Sometimes a discovery
brings back wonderful memories
you've kept in your heart.

A shell from the beach
is a tiny souvenir
of your great joy
in discovering the sea...

One pressed flower
recalls the happy hours you shared
with someone you like.

From things forgotten
you can find for yourself
what others treasured long ago...

The soldier's courage
in a tarnished medal...

The farmer's hope
in a few grains of wheat

And grandmother's love
in her faded shawl.

Do you remember
when you first picked up
a sparkling stone?

Or when you passed
   a haunted house all alone?

It's fun to find

  you've done a task well...

Or come upon a spring flower...

Or quietly enjoyed a solitary hour.

But one day when you find
someone who has been
looking for you...

Love is the most beautiful
discovery of all...
one that is meant
to be shared by two...

...and your heart will be
filled with joy when you
discover someone wonderful
at the very same time
someone wonderful discovers
YOU!